A Hard Nut To Crack

Boomer's Tales: Book 2

by Christine Isley-Farmer

WANDERING IN THE WORDS PRESS

Published by Wandering in the Words Press

WANDERING
IN THE WORDS
PRESS

Print ISBN: 978-1-7360927-4-3
Digital ISBN: 978-1-7360927-5-0
First Edition

For Margaret—sister, wife, mom, grammy, educator—loved by all who know her

1.

Disappearance

I jumped up on my hind legs and yipped, "Throw it!"

"Fetch!" Chloe said. The fuzzy red ball whizzed over my head.

My tail wiggle-waggled; I ran to get my favorite toy.

"Drop it!" she said when I brought it back to her. I placed it at her feet.

"Sorry, boy! This has to be a short game." Chloe gave me a treat. "Mrs. Lee wanted me to stay after school to g-give me some music for the end-of-the-year convocation."

Nana Weathers looked out the door and called, "Hey, you two, come in now. Dinner's almost ready."

"Boomer, I'll race you to the door," Chloe said.

Okay, but we know who's going to win. Four paws are always better than two.

When we got inside, Chloe went to wash her hands. The doorbell rang. Excited, I yipped.

"It's okay, Boomer. I've got it," Nana Weathers said.

When she opened the door, Robbie, our friend, shouted, "Hoppy's gone! I've looked everywhere, but I can't find him. Mom went to the grocery store, and while she was gone, I let Hoppy out to potty in the backyard. I went back in the house for a few minutes to finish up some homework on the computer. When I came back outside and called him, he didn't come. The fence gate was open."

Chloe came out of the bathroom. "W-What's wrong?" she asked.

Robbie told her and added, "When Mom returned, she helped me look for Hoppy. We went through the neighborhood shouting his name and whistling. No luck. Now it's getting dark, and I'm really worried." Robbie pulled out a striped piece of paper from his pocket. "I found this candy wrapper on the ground outside the fence. I don't eat this kind of candy. Why would it be on the ground?"

He handed it to Nana Weathers. She said, "Boomer, come." She put the wrapper to my sniffer and let me sniff, sniff. I smelled Chloe's favorite. She loved anything with chocolate—like chocolate cake, chocolate brownies, and chocolate sprinkles on top of ice cream. I also smelled Robbie, grass, and a human I didn't know. Nana Weathers showed the wrapper to Chloe and asked, "Do *you* eat this kind of candy?"

"No, Nana."

"Well, Boomer's gotten a good sniff, which may prove useful. I'm going to put this away in a safe place for now."

I padded after Nana Weathers into the kitchen. She reached into the drawer where she kept sandwich baggies and put the wrapper into one.

"Boomer, I'm going to put this wrapper on the top shelf of this cabinet so it doesn't accidentally get thrown away. Let's go see if we can give Robbie some reassurance about Hoppy. He's so upset."

When we walked back into the hallway, I heard Chloe say, "I'm sorry about Hoppy. I want to h-help you find him."

Leaping up on my hind legs, I yipped, "Me too!"

Nana Weathers said, "Robbie, we all want to help you find Hoppy. I know how upsetting it is when a pet is missing. When I was a girl, my yellow-striped tabby cat, Pinky, disappeared for two weeks. I looked and looked for him. One day I was out riding my bicycle around the high school with my best friend when I heard a loud meow. Pinky came up to me like I'd been the one who was lost and was now found."

Chloe laughed. Then she said to Robbie, "I've got an idea. Since tomorrow is S-Saturday, talk to your parents about all of you c-coming over to our house for a b-breakfast meeting. We can make a plan for finding Hoppy if he isn't home by morning."

"Yes, we'll form an official Hoppy search party," Nana Weathers said.

Robbie smiled. "Thanks. I knew you'd help. That's why I came over. Although Hoppy is frisky, I don't think he'd run away, even if the fence gate was open."

2.

Questions

I woke up to clouds and rain. They made me even sadder about Hoppy. After Chloe had taken her bath, and Nana Weathers her shower, the rain stopped and the sun came out.

The phone rang. "I bet it's Robbie," Chloe said. She ran to pick up Nana Weathers's phone on the hallway table.

When she'd finished talking to Robbie, Chloe came into the kitchen. "Hoppy hasn't come home," she said. "Robbie and his p-parents have to go to Ella's gymnastics c-competition this morning, but they'll come by when it's over."

"Let's work on some ideas, and when they arrive, we can ask them to add theirs to our list," Nana Weathers said. "While you were on the phone, I began whipping up some pancake batter."

Nana Weathers reached up, opened a cabinet door, and took out a small bag. When she opened the bag and shook those little brown bits into the bowl, they smelled like the chocolate on the candy wrapper I'd sniffed.

"Chloe, we are all sad about Hoppy," Nana Weathers said. "But we need to keep our energy up. That way we can come up with some good ideas about how to find him. These chocolate chip pancakes with butter and maple syrup should do the trick." Looking at me, Nana Weathers added, "Chocolate isn't good for dogs, so I put some small pieces of chicken in your bowl on top of your kibble."

While we were eating, Nana Weathers said, "I've been thinking about Hoppy's disappearance. I believe he was taken by someone who planned it. I don't think it was a coincidence that Hoppy disappeared at the same time Robbie went back into the house."

"Nana, that would m-mean that whoever took Hoppy had been watching the Goodson's backyard. They were waiting for the right m-moment."

She's right, I thought.

"There are woods behind the Goodson's fence, so someone could've possibly hidden there to observe comings and goings," Nana Weathers said.

"How could anyone take Hoppy, Nana? He's much too f-feisty."

Chloe had seen Hoppy in action. She knew he would snap, growl, and bite anyone who tried to take him. She'd seen how he almost chewed off Joey's pant leg when Joey and Ezra had been mean to her and Robbie in the park.

While they continued to talk, I thought about Chloe and the talent show we were in together. I'd helped her by being brave enough to sing for Robbie and Hoppy one afternoon after school in our music room. Then I'd helped her again at the talent show. After the show was over and we were back at our house, I'd yipped to Hoppy, "I did what was best for the team." Robbie and Hoppy were a team and our best friends. I wanted to do my best for them too.

I went to the back door and rubbed my sniffer on the bell hanging from the doorknob to let Nana Weathers know I needed to potty. When she came to let me out, I yipped, "Just let anyone try to take me. I may be small, but my yip is big."

She laughed and said, "After the talent show, Boomer, your yip earned you bragging rights."

***

In the yard, sniff, sniff, sniffing around for the right spot, I heard noise above me in the trees. Suddenly, a branch fell, just missing my head. A tiny voice squeaked, "You won't get away with it." I looked up. Two gray things with furry tails ran and leapt from branch to branch. The first furry thing squeaked again, "Give me back *my* nut! I found it first."

Mommy had always taught my sisters and me that stealing wasn't right. If we got into a fight over a toy that had suddenly disappeared, she'd yip, "Hard feelings are not easy to mend once you've stolen something from a friend." I raised my sniffer and yipped at the furry things.

Nana Weathers had come to the door in time to hear me yip. She came out into the yard and looked up at what was happening. She touched her silver ring. A stream of light shot out, surprising the furry thing being chased.

The light hit the big nut in between the furry thing's teeth. The nut broke into pieces and fell from its mouth. The pieces hit me in the eyes.

"Ouch! Heaps of doggy biscuits," I yipped. "That hurt."

Nana Weathers said, "Sorry! Next time, I'll remember to blow the pieces away."

The chaser's voice squeaked, "I don't know how that happened, but I owe you a word of thanks. Humphrey is always stealing from me and other squirrels. He'd rather steal than gather nuts, seeds, and berries like the rest of us. We're tired of it. Pardon me. I'm being rude. My name is Pipkin. Who might I ask are you?"

"Boomer and Nana Weathers," I yipped.

Nana Weathers said, "Nice to meet you, Pipkin."

When Nana Weathers yipped his name, Pipkin leapt up, flipped, and landed on his tiny feet. "Jumping pinecones!" he squeaked.

"I need to go back into the house now," Nana Weathers said. "Boomer, I'll leave the door open. Come back in when you're ready. The Goodsons arrived a few minutes ago."

"That streak of light came from her hand and struck the nut in Humphrey's mouth," Pipkin squeaked. "How did she do that?"

"Nana Weathers has special powers she uses to help people and animals. Those powers allow her to understand you and me. The silver ring on her finger makes these things happen. I live with her and Chloe, her granddaughter. Chloe doesn't have a silver ring or Nana Weathers's powers, but she and I understand each other without them."

"Ripe mulberries!" Pipkin squeaked. "That's some story in a nutshell."

"Nana Weathers would have stayed longer," I yipped, "but my best dog friend, Hoppy, has been missing since yesterday. We think he was stolen by someone who'd been watching his yard. He lives not too far away from here in a big white house on the corner of his street. Chloe loves the mailbox with leaves painted on it that's in the front. She asked Nana Weathers if we could get one like it. There's a fence in the backyard in front of some woods."

"Acorns aplenty!" Pipkin squeaked. "I think I know where that is! Maybe I can help. I have a network of squirrel friends who live in that neighborhood. I'll ask around to find out if any of them saw anything unusual yesterday."

"Thanks, Pipkin. That'd be great." Turning to pad back into the house, I thought, *I hope Pipkin can help us.*

3.
Networking

When I got back inside, everyone was sitting at the dining room table. Chloe had called and asked her friend Shannon, the flute player from the talent show, to come over too. Nana Weathers had her new laptop open. Why she calls it a laptop, I don't know. It never sits in her lap like I sometimes do.

Nana Weathers put her fingers on the black keys like she does when she plays the piano and said, "Robbie thinks it might be good to hang some flyers in our neighborhoods with Hoppy's picture and his dad's contact numbers."

"We'll work on those tomorrow," Mr. Goodson said. "I'll get them printed up at work on Monday. If the children are willing to post them, that would help."

"I'll help hang some flyers in my neighborhood," Shannon said.

"I think it might also be a good idea to post a notice in the *Daily Examiner*," said Nana Weathers. "If Hoppy is found, the person who finds him will have a way to contact you."

Mrs. Goodson said, "I'll post a picture of Hoppy on my Facebook page. I see posts all the time about missing pets with requests to share those posts. I'll contact some of my friends who'll be happy to share the information on their pages too. The idea is to spread the word far and wide, isn't it?"

"Thanks, Mom," Robbie said.

Robbie's sister, Ella, said, "I can hang some posters up in the middle and high school hallways and pass along the news to my friends too."

"I'll call the animal shelter to see if Hoppy might have been found and turned in," said

Nana Weathers. "Does Hoppy have a micro-chip?"

"Yes, he does," replied Mrs. Goodson. "Dr. Snow advised us to have one implanted when we first took him to be examined."

"Good," said Nana Weathers. "It'll be easy to prove you're Hoppy's family when he's found."

"I'll ride my bike over on Monday to Dr. Snow's office and ask him to post a flyer," Robbie said.

Nana Weathers stood up from the table and walked over to me. "Meanwhile, Boomer may have a way to help too," she said. "Remember, we have the candy wrapper. It might prove helpful in the end if we still haven't found Hoppy. What do you say, Boomer?"

I yipped, "I'm all in on this one. I want my buddy back."

***

After the Goodsons and Shannon left, I wanted to go outside again in case Pipkin had returned with news. As I padded and sniffed around, I heard squirrel noises. Looking up, I saw Pipkin and another squirrel, not Humphrey, sitting on one of the lower branches.

"Tsik," Pipkin squeaked. "I may have some news about your friend. This is Eldredge, chief chatterer and carrier of news in our tree network. He says he heard by way of branch gossip someone on a bike was seen in Hoppy's neighborhood the afternoon he went missing. According to his source, a squirrel in that network saw a rider on a bike with a basket on the back. There was a bag in it. The chatterer thought she heard sounds coming from the bag."

I yipped, "That must've been Hoppy. He's small enough to fit in a bike basket. Do you have anything else, Eldredge?"

"She didn't get a good look at the rider, because she had to scurry to avoid being hit by the speeding bike. She did report that the biker had on a helmet with a visor. She couldn't see a face."

I yipped, "Before I share your news with Nana Weathers, I'd like you to ask your network if they can find out any more information. Would you and your friends be willing to continue to help us? If they see that bike again, would they follow it?"

"Cracked nuts and seeds," Pipkin squeaked. "You can be sure we will! You helped us out with Humphrey. Since that nut in his mouth cracked into pieces, he's stopped trying to steal from us. I hope he may have finally learned his lesson."

Pipkin and Eldredge ran up the tree, wiggle-waggling their furry tails. *I hope the squirrel network sees the biker again*, I thought.

4.
Pet Friend

Everyone at the planning meeting had been doing something to find Hoppy. Chloe, Shannon, and Robbie had gone from door to door in nearby neighborhoods asking about Hoppy. But so far, no good news.

After school one afternoon, Chloe, Shannon, and I were upstairs in Chloe's bedroom. I was listening as they talked about the upcoming festival at New Hope Elementary School. The festival was to raise money for students to go to a summer music camp. From downstairs Nana Weathers called, "I need to do some errands, one of which is to get dog food from the pet store for Boomer. Could you girls go into Pet

Friend for me while I run the other errands on my list? They won't take long. You can bring Boomer along."

On our way, they talked about the slow progress in finding Hoppy. When Nana Weathers pulled the car up to Pet Friend, she said, "We have to be patient and remain optimistic that we'll get some good news soon. I'll be back in twenty minutes. Meet me back here."

Inside the store, Chloe and Shannon got a shopping cart; Chloe placed me in it. As we went up the aisle, people with their kids stopped and said, "What a cute dog! Can we pet him?"

I loved the attention, but as we got near the food section, the smell made me start to drool. Whenever my sisters and I ate our food too fast, Mommy would yip, "A drooling puppy may look more mad than cute."

"Hello there, Chloe and Boomer," a familiar voice said. Bob, our dog obedience trainer, was putting bags of dog food on shelves. "What brings you here today?"

"We're here to p-pick up food for Boomer," Chloe said. "This is my friend Shannon. Shannon, this is Bob. He t-trained Boomer and Hoppy."

"Nice to meet you, Shannon," Bob said. "Chloe, I'm used to seeing you here with Robbie and Hoppy. How are they?"

While Chloe told Bob about Hoppy, I thought about how Hoppy and I had met in Pet Friend. He'd kicked me while running away from Robbie, and he almost got hurt for misbehaving. But after our first meeting, he and I had become best friends. We'd teamed up at our graduation from dog obedience school to teach a lesson to Peanut, the Chihuahua who had turned out to be our class bully.

"I'm sorry to hear this news," Bob said. "I hope you find him soon. Bring by some of those flyers you made, and I'll hang them around the store. You never know who might see Hoppy's picture and remember having seen him somewhere."

Chloe said, "Thanks, Bob."

Just as we were about to leave, Bob said, "I don't know if this is a coincidence or not, but Hoppy's disappearance reminds me that the store recently had some minor theft issues. On Friday, a leash, collar, and muzzle went missing. A few toys and a couple of bags of dog biscuits were gone too. It's very unusual for us to have thefts. We don't have detectors at the doors, but the manager is worried and has notified the regional office about the problem. I don't know if this relates to Hoppy, but the timing seems to coincide with his disappearance. The store has front and back entrance cameras, but lately the front entrance camera has been having some problems. The only odd thing we saw from the backdoor camera was a child about your age, Chloe, possibly a boy, carrying a small backpack. The child left the store wearing a bike helmet with a visor."

When I heard this, I thought about what Pipkin had told me. Eldredge's story about a biker and the bag *must* be linked to the store thefts. I needed to talk to Pipkin and Eldredge again as soon as possible.

Could the Pet Friend biker and the squirrel's biker be the same?

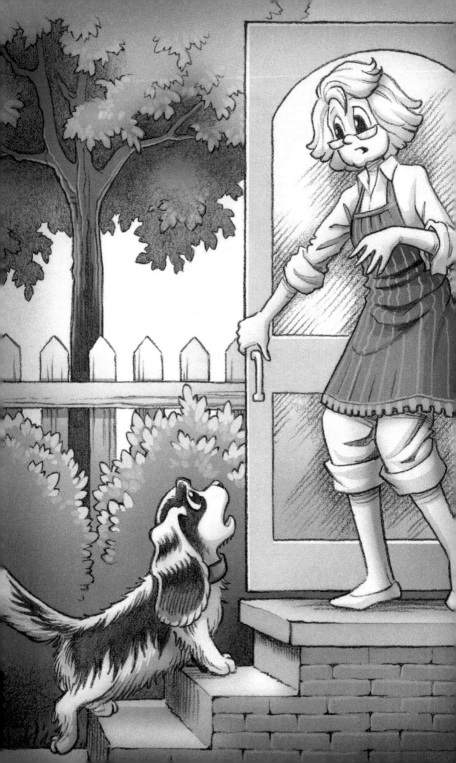

5.

Wounded

In the car, Chloe told Nana Weathers about the pet store thefts. When we arrived home, Chloe asked Nana Weathers for her phone. She and Shannon went upstairs to call Robbie and give him the news. I wanted to go outside to see if Pipkin was around and tell him what I'd learned. I rubbed my sniffer on the bell. Nana Weathers let me out. "Is there something on your mind, Boomer?" she asked. "I know you miss Hoppy, but you aren't acting like yourself."

I yipped, "I'm trying to put the pieces of this bone together." As I ran out into the yard, I thought about what I'd already learned. I remembered what Mommy had yipped about solving a problem. She'd bark, "If all you have is questions, it's because you need to diggity, diggity, dig up more answers."

I heard thumping and squirrels chattering. Pipkin and some of his friends ran down the tree. Before I could yip at Pipkin, he squeaked, "Help us, Boomer! Eldredge's tail has just been bitten off by a dog. It's bleeding, and Eldredge is chattering wildly."

"Okay," I barked, "but I need to get Nana Weathers. She'll know what to do."

Barking, I ran to the back door. Nana Weathers came running. "What's all the commotion about?"

"Pipkin's friend, Eldredge, is hurt. He's been bitten by a dog."

"Let's go right away," she said.

Pipkin and his friends were sitting on top of our wooden fence when Nana Weathers came out. Her ring glowing, Nana Weathers said, "Lead the way."

We found Eldredge lying on his side tsiking. Luckily, he'd been able to get through the fence boards, but all of his tail had not. Some of it was missing. Most of the fur was gone, and the end of it was red.

Nana Weathers bent down. She said to the squirrels, "You can help Eldredge if you sit behind me and close your eyes."

The squirrels obeyed. She rubbed her ring. The light from it got brighter. A white circle appeared over Eldredge's tail. Nana Weathers hummed as her hands moved over that circle of light.

When she removed her hands, the end of Eldredge's tail was no longer as red. She said to the squirrels, "You can open your eyes now." When the squirrels opened their eyes, they chattered and thumped their feet.

"Great acorns! Eldredge isn't tsiking anymore; his tail looks better," squeaked Pipkin.

"Although Eldredge's tail is better, he's going to need some antibiotics for any possible infection," said Nana Weathers. "He needs to see Boomer's vet, Dr. Snow. Boomer and I'll take him first thing in the morning. Eldredge can stay with us tonight. We'll take good care of him."

Nana Weathers took off the apron she was wearing and laid it on the ground. Lifting Eldredge, she placed him on it and covered all but his little head. As she picked him up, she said, "I'll make sure Eldredge is safe and warm tonight."

Pipkin and his buddies ran back up into the trees. Leaping from branch to branch, they followed us home. As we went in the back door, Nana Weathers turned and waved. I barked and wagged my tail. "Eldredge is going to be as good as new."

I hoped I was right about that. He was the chief chatterer and carrier of news in the squirrel network.

6.
Clue

In the morning, Nana Weathers and I took Eldredge to see Dr. Snow. While we were waiting for him to examine Eldredge, Nana Weathers talked to Charlene, Dr. Snow's assistant. Charlene asked her, "Have you found Hoppy yet?"

"No, we're still hoping for some good news. It's been almost a week and still no answers."

I hung my head; I'd not shared with her all I'd learned from the squirrels.

"I believe it may have been a child or a teen who took Hoppy," Nana Weathers said. "Robbie found a candy wrapper in the yard near the fence gate. Of course, that wrapper could have blown into the yard, but it's our only clue, aside from some disappearing items from Pet Friend."

Charlene said, "Hmm . . . yesterday afternoon a boy came in. He wanted to talk to Dr. Snow, but I told him Dr. Snow was in surgery. I asked him if there was anything I could do to help. He told me his dog was sick and needed some medicine. I told him Dr. Snow would have to examine his dog first before he could prescribe any medication."

I barked and wiggle-waggled my tail. "This *may* be Hoppy."

Nana Weathers asked, "Was the child with a parent?"

"No, he was by himself."

"Can you give me a description of him?"

"He's shorter than Chloe, skinny, has blond hair, freckles, and blue eyes. He looked at the flyer we'd posted with Hoppy's picture and rushed out of here. I followed him, thinking a parent might be waiting in a car. But he climbed on a silver and green bike and rode away."

Dr. Snow came out from the examination room with Eldredge. He said, "This little fellow's going to be fine; his injury is minor. It looks like you knew what to do to reduce the chances of infection. I'm amazed the wound on his tail has already begun to heal. I've given him an antibiotic shot just to make sure, so he should be up and running around in another day or two. His tail won't grow back but his fur will. He should soon be his old self again."

Hearing that news, Eldredge chattered, "Poppin' and crackin' hickory nuts!"

After we got home, I told Nana Weathers everything I'd learned from Pipkin and Eldredge. She said, "Boomer, you've developed into quite a little detective. We've still got some fact-finding to do, but a solution may not be as difficult as we think. An all-out neighborhood squirrel alert is now in order. Sometimes a thief will return to the scene of the crime. Can you talk to our little friends and tell them how important it is for them to remain watchful, especially since Eldredge may need to recover for a few more days?"

"Eldredge will get the word out," I yipped. "He's chattered that he's feeling good enough to leap back into action."

7.

Close Call

Eldredge, acting like himself again, was able to join his friends before we had our breakfasts. When Chloe got home from school, she said, "Nana, Robbie's aunt is s-sick. Her husband is out of town, so Mr. and Mrs. Goodson want to help with the ch-children and stay with her until she's feeling better. Robbie wants to know if he can s-stay here since Ella is going to stay with one of her f-friends. Mrs. Goodson is going to call you."

"That's fine, Chloe. I'll call Mr. and Mrs. Goodson right now. We'll go and pick up Robbie so they can get to her sister's house as soon as possible."

Back home, Nana Weathers cooked dinner while Robbie and Chloe talked at the table about Hoppy. When Nana Weathers placed Robbie's plate of food in front of him, he sat there looking down at it. This was not the Robbie I knew. He was usually a chow hound like me and Hoppy.

Between tiny bites of mashed potatoes and roast beef, Robbie said, "We've got to find Hoppy soon. I hope he's not sick. Maybe this kid at Dr. Snow's office is not the same as the one who snatched Hoppy. Even though we've got a description, there're lots of kids in New Hope who look like that."

"Yes, but we know he rides a s-silver and green bike," said Chloe. "I wonder if he rides that b-bike to school. Let's check the bike racks tomorrow."

Nana Weathers served more green beans to Chloe. "Since you and Robbie are busy with after-school activities tomorrow, Boomer and I'll go over to the school before it lets out. We'll keep an eye out for any bikers on silver and green bikes. Afterward, I'll need to stop by the dry cleaners to pick up some things."

Chloe, looking at Robbie, said, "We should be f-finished by 4:30, so we'll stand outside the school's f-front door and wait for you."

"I should be back before then, so don't hurry," Nana Weathers said.

"Nana, do you have any of that ch-chocolate meringue pie left? I'd like a piece, and I bet Robbie would too."

"I do, and I have some new liver treats for Boomer."

"Liver!" exclaimed Robbie. "Yuck! I hate it!"

Nana Weathers laughed. "That's okay, Robbie. Chloe doesn't like it either. But liver treats are high on the treat list for dogs. Let's see if Boomer will roll over for one."

When she went to my treat jar, I was ready. She held the treat over my sniffer and said, "Boomer, roll over!"

I rolled over not once but twice and yipped too. Robbie and Chloe laughed and clapped.

Nana Weathers looked at them and smiled. "I think Boomer deserves more than one. Don't you?"

After dessert, Robbie and Chloe went upstairs to do homework. I padded over to Nana Weathers. "I'll yip to Pipkin and Eldredge to go with some of their friends to the school tomorrow afternoon to watch out for any riders on silver and green bikes. Maybe they'll be able to follow too."

"Good idea, Boomer."

Once I was outside, I yipped and Pipkin came.

"My friends and I are grateful for what you and Nana Weathers did for Eldredge," squeaked Pipkin. "I've always been curious about living in a human house. When I tried to chatter with Eldredge about it, he squeaked, 'Empty nutshells! I was out of it.'"

I yipped, "Inside our house are lots of rooms with furniture. There's a kitchen where Nana Weathers cooks food. She and Chloe sit at a table to eat. I eat from a food bowl on the floor. But my favorite room is the music room where Nana Weathers, Chloe, and I make music. Our house is good because it's warm when it's cold outside and cool when it's hot."

"Some squirrels, like those in my network, build large nests in trees. Other networks live in tree holes and underground," squeaked Pipkin. "One time, my curiosity about human houses almost got me into a too-tight tree hole. I'd found my way into a big room in the top of a house. I guess I made too much noise chewing on some wood to keep my teeth in shape, scratching, and leaping around. I heard a door open and scurried to hide as fast as I could."

My ears perked up. "What happened?"

"I'd heard chatter from other squirrels about narrowly escaping from rooms in tops of houses, so I didn't dare make a sound. A big man came into the room with a box. He put it down and left. I came out and looked at that box from a distance. It had an opening where a door should be; there was something inside.

Smelling something wasn't right, I got out of there as fast as I could scurry."

"I'm glad you got out okay. I don't like it when friends get hurt," I yipped. "I hope Hoppy is safe and we find him soon."

Running up a tree, Pipkin squeaked, "Eldredge will get the chatter out to our network. We'll be at the school tomorrow afternoon ready to scurry."

***

Nana Weathers parked the car where she usually waited for Chloe. I was in the back seat looking out the window. I could see squirrels up in the trees. The school bell rang. Kids carrying backpacks ran out the entrance.

"I see our friends have arrived. A few of them are already on top of one of the school buses," Nana Weathers said. "I gave Chloe my phone this morning. She and Robbie checked the bike rack during lunch. She called to tell me three silver and green bikes were locked to the rack; all three had baskets on the back. Maybe we'll have some luck today."

"I hope we can see their faces," I yipped.

"Boomer, you're one smart doggy detective. I'm going to get out of the car now and see if I can get a better look at the bike racks. So far, I've seen two children ride away on bikes that weren't silver and green. You stay here for now. I'll leave one of the windows down. If you see anything, bark. I'll have no trouble recognizing it's you." Smiling, she walked away.

I watched as she got close to the first bus with squirrels on top. Kids were getting on it.

Deciding I wanted a better look, I stuck my head out the window. The door of the first bus shut. I knew it was about to leave. The squirrels on top of it began to leap off, but one of them, short-tailed Eldredge, remained on top. I barked over and over, "Eldredge, get off the top of the bus!"

The school bus, beginning to roll, sped up. Eldredge had not made it off and was slipping and sliding. A kid on a bike raced in front of the bus. Nana Weathers, having heard my bark, saw what was happening too. She rubbed her ring, and a wall of light appeared in front of the bus as it started to leave. It screeched to a stop.

Making her whistle mouth, she blew Eldredge up into a tree branch. The kid on the bike rode off.

When Nana Weathers got back into the car, she winked and said, "That was a close call. The bus driver reacted quickly, so the child was in no danger. Poor little Eldredge was losing his footing and would have fallen off. When you barked, I looked back at the car, so I didn't see the children's faces clearly enough before they put on their helmets. But I'm pretty sure they were both boys, and I saw the color of their hair. The boy on the silver and green bike who raced in front of the bus has blond hair. The other boy who got on the second silver and green bike has blond hair too. The remaining silver and green bike is still locked to the rack."

8.

Dream

Chloe and Robbie were waiting for us outside the school entrance. When they were in the car, Nana Weathers told them about the blond-haired boy on a silver and green bike who was almost hit by the bus and a second blond boy who also rode off on a silver and green bike. She left out the part about saving Eldredge.

Nana Weathers said, "The situation is a bit more complex now that we know two of the boys who have silver and green bikes are both blond. Since I had to leave to go to pick up the dry cleaning, I couldn't wait for the last boy."

"Problem solved," Robbie said. "A red-haired boy named Stuart, who is on my basketball drill team, came out of the school entrance with me and Chloe. He got on the last silver and green bike."

When dinner was over, Nana Weathers told Robbie and Chloe to go do their homework while she and I took a walk across the street in the park. She said we'd all talk when we got back.

Sitting down on the park bench, she said, "Boomer, you know this ring helps me perform magic, but it, like music, also helps people and animals heal. At the talent show, I know you saw the white light appear above Chloe's head when she sang. I didn't make that happen. Chloe was able to do this herself. Like my grandmother and me, she has a gift. Although she's still young, she's seeing messages in her dreams. Last night she came into my room and told me a dream she'd had about Hoppy. She told it to me like one of her poems."

Alone and muzzled in a dark shed,
A hard and cold floor his only bed,
Water dish set to his right side,
Two back legs to a leash are tied.
With a rubber toy his only friend,
Hoppy waits for his sad heart to mend.
He'd give up basketball and food alright,
For one glimpse of Robbie's face in light.

When Nana Weathers finished the poem, we heard tsiking above us in the trees. Pipkin and Eldredge came scurrying down. Pipkin sat on top of the park bench next to Nana Weathers. Short-tailed Eldredge climbed on top of her shoulder.

Eldredge chattered in her ear. "Merry berries! That was some flight today! Not even a flying squirrel could top that."

She laughed and asked, "Were your squirrel friends able to follow the bikers?"

"Yes, they set up a clever branch-to-branch network and were able to follow both boys," squeaked Pipkin.

Eldredge chattered, "Our network needed to split up to follow both boys, so we didn't have enough squirrels to wait for the last biker."

"That's okay. Robbie told us he has red hair," Nana Weathers said.

"The boy who almost got hit by the bus stopped near Hoppy's house and looked around for a few minutes before riding on," Pipkin squeaked. "This gave us a chance to catch our breaths. We followed him to a house with a car in the driveway. There's a wooden shed in the backyard, but the windows are covered. There's a lock on the door."

Nana Weathers said, "Chloe saw a shed in her dream."

"The other boy we followed lives near the first boy," Eldredge chattered. "There's a wooden shed in his backyard too. Some of our friends jumped down onto that shiny, slippery roof and almost fell off. There's a covered window, and the shed has a lock."

Nana Weathers said, "Thank you. Tell your friends how much we appreciate their information and ask them to please keep a lookout on those houses and sheds."

"Crackin' nuts and mulberries," Eldredge chattered as he leapt from Nana Weathers's shoulder to the tree trunk.

Pipkin squeaked, "We've already set up a watch schedule." He followed Eldredge up into the branches.

When Nana Weathers and I returned to the house, she shouted up the stairs, "Chloe! Robbie! Come down. We've got plans to make before tomorrow's school festival."

9.
School Festival

My eyes opened. Chloe was out of bed putting on her clothes. She said, "Wake up, sleepy head. It's time to get going." She knocked on Robbie's door.

"Coming!" he said.

The three of us ran down the stairs. When we got to the kitchen, Nana Weathers said, "Chloe, let Boomer out to potty." I wondered if any of my squirrel friends might be in the trees, but none of them were there.

Nana Weathers filled my dish when I came back in, but she hadn't prepared breakfast for Chloe and Robbie. "There'll be plenty of food this morning at the festival," she said to them.

"Let's wait until we get there and buy something. June Seever bakes the best blueberry and chocolate muffins I've ever eaten. You two go on out to the car. I'll be right along with Boomer."

Nana Weathers went to the cabinet and pulled out the baggie with the candy wrapper in it. She called me over and held the wrapper to my sniffer. "I'll take this along today, Boomer, just in case you need another sniff or two. Maybe you'll recognize that scent at the festival."

In the car, Chloe said, "I hope Shannon and I will be chosen to go to the music camp this summer."

"Chloe, I'm so proud of you," said Nana Weathers. "You're my talented granddaughter who has a lot of courage. I believe you and Shannon have a good chance of being awarded scholarships to Camp Resound."

"Hear that, Boomer?" Chloe said. "If Shannon and I are chosen, m-maybe you can come and be a camp mascot."

I'd been trying to listen, but the smell of chocolate cake, brownies, and pecan pie that Nana Weathers had baked and packed in the bag sitting next to me in the back seat had my sniffer's full attention. Drooling, I licked my chops and yipped, "That sounds like fun."

When we arrived at the festival, we met up with Robbie's parents. Mrs. Goodson said, "I didn't have time to bake, so I picked up a carrot and strawberry cake from the bakery. My sister is feeling better now, so Robbie can come home with us afterwards. We'd like to thank you and invite you over for a cookout next Saturday evening. Peter will grill his super-duper burgers with, as he says, 'all the fixins.' Hopefully, we'll have Hoppy back by then."

"I hope so too," Nana Weathers said. "I'd like to bring some of my baked beans to add to your cookout if it's okay."

"Celia, you're one of the best cooks in this town. We'd love for you to bring your beans."

***

After eating their muffins, Chloe said, "Robbie, let's split up and talk to the kids and p-parents here. We might hear something about Hoppy."

"That's a good idea. Meet you back here."

"Chloe, hold up," Nana Weathers said. "I'm going to let Boomer smell this wrapper once more before you two take off."

While Chloe and I walked around, I pointed my sniffer in all directions.

Chloe said, "There's Elvis. Mr. Brown sometimes brings him to events for us to ride. I've never ridden a d-donkey, but it looks like fun."

As Chloe and I looked at the people and kids waiting to ride Elvis, my sniffer caught the scent I'd just sniffed on the candy wrapper. I pulled at my leash. When I stopped in front of a blond-haired boy, Chloe said, "Hi, Timmy and Mrs. Braxton. It's a great day for the f-festival, isn't it?"

"It really is," said Mrs. Braxton. "I'm happy the school is raising money for such a worthy—"

"C'mon, Mom," Timmy said. "This line's too long. Let's do something else. I want to jump on the trampoline." Timmy ran off with Mrs. Braxton chasing after him.

"B-Boomer, did you smell something?"

I pointed my sniffer up at Chloe and yipped.

"C'mon. I see Robbie talking to C-Collin and Mike."

Out of breath, Chloe asked them, "D-Do you know Timmy B-Braxton?"

"No, not really," Robbie said. "Timmy is quiet like me and doesn't say much."

"Yeah," Collin added. "He keeps to himself, and if you ask him a question, he sometimes acts like he doesn't hear you."

"Timmy used to be friendlier," said Mike, "but the last few weeks he's been avoiding me."

Chloe told Robbie and the other boys about how I'd stopped right next to Timmy standing in line with his mom. She said, "He'll usually talk to me, b-but this time he ran off."

"Some of the boys Timmy used to hang around with have said he's been keeping to himself lately," Mike said.

Chloe asked, "Do you know where he lives?"

"I think he lives on Elm or Poplar Street," Collin said.

"Robbie, "Let's go! N-Nana needs to hear this."

Nana Weathers was standing at the dessert tables talking with friends. When she saw the three of us running toward her, she stepped away. "N-Nana, we know who m-may have taken H-Hoppy. We think it was T-Timmy Braxton."

Robbie said, "Collin told us Timmy lives on Elm or Poplar Street. I'm going to find my parents."

"Hold on, Robbie," Nana Weathers said. "You don't know for sure Timmy is the thief, and you don't know the exact address. I think we need to be careful, take our time, and find out more information."

"B-But, Nana, Boomer pulled me to him. I j-just know it's him." Stopping to take a breath, Chloe said, "I have an idea how to find out f-for sure if Timmy stole Hoppy. I'll try to get him to talk to me during recess on Monday. If you let me t-take your phone to school, I'll ask Shannon to take a picture of Timmy and me. We can take that ph-photo and show it to Charlene. She'll know if T-Timmy is the boy who came to Dr. Snow's office."

Robbie said, "Chloe, that's a great idea. Can I go with you to show the photo to Charlene?"

Chloe nodded.

"Maybe we can run by Pet Friend too," Robbie said. "Bob or someone else may have seen him in there if he took off his helmet."

"Robbie, Boomer, and I will pick up you and Chloe after school on Monday," Nana Weathers said.

10.
Search

Monday arrived. Nana Weathers and I dropped Chloe off at school. "Boomer, let's drive over to Elm and Poplar Streets. I brought your leash."

I yipped, "Our friends must have been busy watching the houses. I haven't seen them in our backyard."

"Let's take a walk up and down those two streets," Nana Weathers said. She stopped the car in front of a house. "Since Elm Street is closer to the Goodson's house, let's walk down it first. I bet our squirrel friends, if they're around, will recognize us."

A few houses away, we heard lots of chattering and tsiking. Looking up, we saw the trees in the yard filled with squirrels. I recognized Eldredge as he ran down from one of the taller trees. He scurried toward us.

I yipped, "Good to see you! We were hoping you'd see us on our walk and show us the houses where the boys stopped."

Eldredge chattered, "Good nuts and seeds! The other boy we were watching has a great big dog, so I had that network relocate to this yard. This is where the other blond-haired boy lives."

"Smart thinking," said Nana Weathers.

"Unfortunately, something happened and we had to leave the yard unwatched," chattered Eldredge. "Humphrey discovered we were away. He and some of his friends raided some of our stashes. We found out only because one of his accomplices let us know. We had to leave to protect what was left of our food. As soon as we saw how much they had stolen from us, we needed to gather more nuts and seeds and dig new stash locations. We didn't get back here until just now."

"You can't survive the cold winter without food," said Nana Weathers. "We appreciate that you came back here to continue your watch. If you hadn't been here, we wouldn't have known this is the house where the blond-haired boy lives."

I yipped, "Did you notice anything while you were still on watch?"

"I stayed behind longer to help with burying nuts, but Pipkin returned here early this morning," Eldredge chattered. "He squeaked that one of the house windows was open. He saw and heard a woman talking to a boy about the importance of doing his homework. Apparently, he hadn't done it yet. Pipkin would be here too, but he's gone to get a little shut-eye after being up all last night and on watch this morning."

Nana Weathers said, "Tell him and your network friends how much we appreciate all they've done. If you can keep a watch on this house just a little longer, it would be helpful."

Chattering, Eldredge ran up a tree in the front yard.

Nana Weathers and I went home for lunch.

***

After she ate and gave me two of my favorite liver treats, she asked, "Boomer, do you feel like singing before we pick up Chloe and Robbie from school?"

Yipping, I ran to the door of the music room. We had not gone in there to make music since Hoppy had gone missing.

Nana Weathers sat down at the piano. I padded over to her side. "Boomer, I know a sad song about missing someone. I'm going to play and sing part of it for you. I'll then repeat that part and you can sing it with me."

When she stopped playing and singing, the light from her ring circled around me. She said, "Now, let's sing this much together."

I felt the warmth of those sparkling lights and sang along with her.

When we finished singing the first part, Nana Weathers said, "Boomer, this song has a good ending because the friend returns. I'll sing and play this last part for you. You'll hear there's a happy ending, because there's a key change to a brighter key. You'll then sing with me."

When I heard Nana Weathers sing the last part of the song, I felt happier. I jumped up on my hind legs and sang the repeat with her as loud as I could.

"Let's sing the whole song now without stopping, Boomer. I'm feeling better too."

After the song ended, Nana Weathers said, "I think we could both use some lap time." She went to her rocking chair and sat. Patting her lap, she invited me to jump up into it. She said, "I feel hopeful Hoppy will soon be found."

I yipped, "Me too."

We sat and rocked until it was time to pick up Chloe and Robbie from school.

***

Chloe and Robbie ran out of the school and jumped into the car. Nana Weathers said, "Let's go to Dr. Snow's office first. Boomer and I'll go in with you so Charlene doesn't think you've shown up out of the blue to ask her questions."

Charlene was talking on the phone, so we sat down to wait until she was free. After she'd finished, she asked, "Did you have an appointment for Boomer? I don't have him down on my calendar for this afternoon."

Chloe and Robbie ran to her desk. "N-No, Boomer d-doesn't have an appointment," Chloe said.

Nana Weathers walked up to the desk and said, "Charlene, we're hoping you can give us some information." She showed Charlene the photo Shannon had taken.

"We want to know if this is the boy who came in asking for medicine for his dog," Robbie said.

Charlene looked at it. "Yes, that's him. Do you think he might have taken Hoppy?"

Robbie replied, "We're not sure yet, but it looks more and more like he did."

We thanked Charlene, told her to tell Dr. Snow why we'd stopped by, and then drove to Pet Friend.

As soon as we walked through the door, we saw Bob. He was hanging dog toys on a rack at the front of the store. When I saw some of the toys were squirrels, I barked, "I don't like seeing my friends hanging there to be shaken and chewed on."

Bob asked, "What's wrong with Boomer to-day?"

"I don't think he likes some of your toys," Nana Weathers replied.

Nana Weathers showed Bob the photo of Timmy.

He said, "I don't recognize him, but if you can wait, I'll take your phone around to a few employees and show the photo to them."

As soon as Bob returned, he said, "Debbie remembers seeing this boy in the store. She said he was alone and looking around. He asked her some questions about dog food and the best kind of toys for dogs. Does this have anything to do with Hoppy?"

"Bob, thank you," said Nana Weathers. "We don't know everything yet, but you've been extremely helpful. We'll pick up some of those liver treats I bought last time I was here. Boomer loves them."

Licking my chops and drooling a little, I thought, *I can't wait to share my new liver treats when we find you, buddy!*

11.

Shed

After we left Pet Friend, Chloe asked, "Can we go to Timmy's house and find out if he has a dog?"

"I think it might be best if I go there alone first," Nana Weathers said. "I'll bake a coconut cake, phone Mrs. Braxton, and ask if I can come by shortly before school is out. At one of the organizational meetings for the festival, she told me she works from home. While I'm there, I can ask her a few questions. If there's a dog in the house, it'll probably bark when I ring the doorbell. One way or another, we'll at least find out if they have a dog. I may be able to find out more about that shed in the backyard too."

Nana Weathers drove me and the coconut cake to the Braxton house. When we pulled up in front of the house, I yipped, "Let me go with you. I'll recognize Hoppy's scent if he's been in the house or is in the shed."

"That's not a good idea right now," Nana Weathers said. "We aren't sure if the Braxtons have a dog and if not, Mrs. Braxton might prefer not to have a dog inside the house. You can help me by keeping your eye out for Timmy. If you see him coming, bark. I'll leave the car windows cracked for fresh air."

She carried the cake with her and rang the doorbell. Mrs. Braxton answered the door. I was sad I didn't hear a barking dog when Mrs. Braxton opened the door to let Nana Weathers in. I started feeling sleepy while I waited, but I perked up my ears when I heard ding, ding, ding, ding, ding. I saw Timmy riding up the street on his bike. He rode it into his backyard. I barked.

When Nana Weathers came out the door, she said, "Goodbye, Helen! I hope you and Timmy enjoy the cake."

Back in the car, she said, "Boomer, I know you're anxious to find out what I learned. I have some things I want to tell you, but I want Chloe, Robbie, and the Goodsons to hear them too. I'll call after dinner and see if it'll be convenient for us to stop by for a visit."

***

After dinner, Chloe and I got in the car with Nana Weathers and drove to the Goodsons.

Before Chloe could ring the doorbell, Robbie opened the door and shouted, "What did you find out?"

Mrs. Goodson called from the living room, "Robbie, please bring our guests in here."

Mr. and Mrs. Goodson and Ella were watching TV, but Mr. Goodson turned it off when we entered the room.

I could smell Hoppy more strongly than when we'd first entered his house. Knowing where his toy basket was, I padded over to it. On top of his toys was his favorite small orange and black basketball that Robbie threw for games of fetch. His ball reminded me of our practice sessions for dog training school. I remembered Chloe saying, "Oops," when she dropped a bag filled with my treats on the ground. Hoppy had run as fast as he could to gobble them up.

Nana Weathers told the Goodsons about her visit with Mrs. Braxton. "Helen told me she and her husband are separated. When Mr. Braxton was offered a relocation to Dallas for his job, they decided it would be a good time to file for divorce. She said she's worried about Timmy. He's having difficulty with his dad being gone. Helen told me Timmy's interest in school and outside activities has stopped. He doesn't ask to bring any friends over to the house or to go play with them."

"Poor boy. It has to be difficult for him and Mrs. Braxton right now," said Mrs. Goodson.

"Yes. She told me she's thinking of selling the house. In her words, 'It's more yard than I can take care of. That shed in the back is a constant reminder of Dan, who kept all his garden tools there. He loves to garden, but I never had time or interest in it,'" said Nana Weathers.

Robbie asked, "Is there a dog?"

"No, but Timmy had been asking Mrs. Braxton for one. She told me he'd been very persistent for a while but hadn't mentioned it lately," Nana Weathers said. "She was hoping he'd lost interest, since it would be inconvenient for Timmy to have one right now."

Chloe said, "N-Nana, we have to go over t-there right now and look in that shed. I s-saw Hoppy in a shed in my dream."

"Chloe told me about her dream. We *have* to go now!" Robbie said. "It's not that dark yet."

"Okay," said Nana Weathers. Giving the Goodsons the address, she said, "Chloe, Boomer, and I will go on ahead."

***

"Chloe, go to the front door and ring the bell," said Nana Weathers. "If there's no answer, check the back door. If there's still no answer, go back to the front yard and wait for the Goodsons. Boomer, you come with me."

I was on my leash, but Nana Weathers let go as soon as I began to yip. I raced ahead to the shed barking. Smelling Hoppy, I jumped up and down scratching at the door.

Nana Weathers said, "Okay, Boomer. Sing for Hoppy to reassure him!" She touched her ring; sparkling lights surrounded me. I stood up on my hind legs and yipped some of the melody from Chloe's song that we'd performed at the talent show. My squirrel friends in the trees started to chatter along with my singing. Pipkin and Eldredge ran down from the trees onto the shed's roof.

"That's enough for now, Boomer," Nana Weathers said, as the sparkling lights disappeared. "Now stand behind me."

She rubbed her ring and raised both hands. Rays of light left her fingers, hitting the lock.

BOOM!

Pipkin and Eldredge jumped. Nana Weathers made her whistle mouth and blew our friends back up into the trees. The pieces from the shed lock went flying too.

Robbie, followed by his parents, Ella, and Chloe, came running toward us. Nana Weathers, picking up pieces of the lock, said, "Robbie should go in first. Chloe, open the door for him."

Robbie ran into the shed. We all gathered around the door. He shouted, "Hoppy! Hoppy! You're really here. Dad, can you come help me untie Hoppy's legs and take off this muzzle?"

Mr. Goodson went into the shed. "C'mon, boy. It's time for you to come home with us," he said.

When Hoppy limped out of the shed with Robbie and Mr. Goodson, he saw me and barked, "Man, that was some kinda big offensive foul in there. I was gettin' so tired of those same old doggy biscuits that I pretended to be sick."

An angry Robbie asked, "Dad, how could someone treat a dog like Hoppy's been treated?"

"Son, I think we need to hear the truth from Timmy about why he stole Hoppy and locked him up in this shed. There really is no good excuse for treating him this way."

A car pulled into the driveway with Mrs. Braxton and Timmy in it. They got out and walked toward us. Timmy looked down at the ground.

"What's going on here?" asked Mrs. Braxton.

Robbie stepped forward and told her the story. Mrs. Braxton looked at Timmy and asked, "What do you have to say for yourself, young man?"

With his head down, Timmy said, "I knew Robbie had a dog, so I'd sometimes go after school on my bike to the woods behind his house and watch him play with Hoppy. I've missed Dad a lot since he moved. When I asked you if I could have a dog, you told me I couldn't. I got mad and took Hoppy."

Nana Weathers told Mrs. Braxton about the missing items from Pet Friend and the visit to Dr. Snow. Mrs. Braxton turned to Timmy and said, "Anger and sadness are never good reasons to steal, Timmy. You and I'll go by the pet store tomorrow after school to talk to the manager." To the Goodsons she said, "I'm so sorry about this." Pulling out her cell phone, she asked Mr. Goodson, "May I have your cell number? I'd like to call you after Timmy and I've had time to talk. He needs some time to think about what he's done."

After Mr. Goodson gave her his number, Mrs. Braxton took Timmy by the hand and led him back to the house. Before going in, Timmy looked back at us.

12.
Happy Endings

My best dog friend and I were together again. Enjoying the sunny day and hoping we'd get one of those burgers on the grill, Hoppy and I padded around his backyard. I could see he was not back to his old self. I yipped, "Hoppy, do you feel like yipping about what happened?"

"Sure, man. I was mindin' my own business when this boy whistled, opened the gate, and threw a meaty bone to me. Now, you know how much I like food, but I don't get that kind of food here. Mrs. Goodson keeps a watch out to make sure everything I get is 'veterinary approved,' as she says. That boy looked okay enough to me, but when I lay down and started chewing on that bone, he threw a bag over me and put me and the bone in it. Next thing I knew, he was running with me in that bag."

"That must've scared you," I yipped.

"It did. I wanted to bark, but I had some of that meaty bone stuck in my throat. I tried to cough it up, but it took a while."

Robbie and Chloe came up to us. Robbie bent down and picked Hoppy up. He said, "I feel so lucky that I got Hoppy back."

"I know," Chloe said. "I don't know what I'd d-do if something like that ever h-happened to Boomer." She picked me up. "I'm so glad the f-four of us are back together again."

***

The phone rang. I heard Nana Weathers say, "Chloe, Boomer, and I can come over to your house tomorrow evening."

When she'd hung up, she went to the music room and opened the door. Chloe was practicing the piano piece Mrs. Lee had given her for convocation.

Nana Weathers said, "Mr. Goodson just called and wants us to come over tomorrow night at 7:30. Mrs. Braxton and Timmy want to meet with all of us."

When everyone had arrived and was seated in the Goodson's living room, Mrs. Braxton said, "Timmy has something he'd like to say to all of you."

Timmy stood up and stepped forward, facing all of us. "It was wrong for me to steal Hoppy, and to steal from Pet Friend too. I'm going to be working at Pet Friend to make up for what I stole. Mom says it's a kind of community service project." Timmy took a big breath. "I shouldn't have tied Hoppy up and muzzled him in our shed. I know now that it was cruel, but I was just so mad at Dad for leaving me and Mom behind." Timmy brushed his hands over his eyes.

Nana Weathers said, "Timmy, you showed you have a good heart when you went to see

Dr. Snow because you thought Hoppy was sick."

Timmy smiled at her and looked at his mom. "I was afraid if I didn't muzzle and tie Hoppy up, he'd get loose and bark."

Timmy walked over to Hoppy, bent down, and said, "I didn't mean to hurt you. I just wanted a special dog like you."

Hoppy looked up at Timmy, slowly wagged his tail, and yipped, "I'll try not to penalize you for that big technical foul."

Mrs. Braxton said, "I've told Timmy we'll go to the animal shelter and adopt a dog when he gets back from visiting his dad this summer.

But first, he has to learn how to take care of one, do his homework, and help me around the house and yard."

Chloe and Robbie looked at one another and together said, "Maybe we can give him some pointers about dog care."

***

After we got home, Chloe went up to her room to finish some homework and get ready for bed. Before padding upstairs after her, Nana Weathers said, "Boomer, let's go outside for your final goodnight potty. I also need to take care of some unfinished business with our squirrel friends."

We walked out the door and stood under our big tree. From her jacket pockets, Nana Weathers removed two big bags of nuts. I heard our friends chattering above us. She opened the bags and threw the nuts on the ground.

"We couldn't have found Hoppy without your help," she said. "I hope this will help replenish the stash Humphrey and his accomplices stole from you."

As Nana Weathers and I turned to walk back to the house, I remembered Hoppy had once yipped how Peanut the Chihuahua was "a hard nut to crack." Hoppy's disappearance had been hard to crack too.

The End

Sniffing Out Funtastic Facts

Eastern Gray Squirrels, like Pipkin, Humphrey, and Eldredge, are native to eastern North America. Oak and hickory forests are their favorite habitats. They build their dens on large tree branches, in hollows of tree trunks, and in abandoned bird nests. In city areas, they can be found in parks and in the backyards of houses. They eat nuts, seeds, berries, buds, and tree flowers. As winter approaches, they bury their food in various locations, but they hide more food than they'll ever eat. With so many food stashes in various locations, they have an excellent sense of smell for finding them. Squirrels communicate using different tail positions, movements, and vocalizations. For more information about Eastern gray squirrels, go to https://kids.nationalgeographic.com/animals/mammals/eastern-gray-squirrel

Flying Squirrels glide from one tree to another with the use of parachute-like membranes called patagia, which stretch from wrist to ankle. Flying squirrels make their nests in abandoned nests of birds and other squirrels and in woodpecker holes. These nests help keep them warm in winter.
For more information about flying squirrels, go to National Wildlife Federation at nwf.org.

<u>Squirrel Activities:</u>

Tsik/Tsiking is a word the author made up for sounds squirrels make. Try listening to squirrels and see if you can have fun making up words for their sounds too.

Chatter as a noun means rapid talk. As a verb, **chattering** means to talk rapidly or, in the case of teeth, to click rapidly.

Scurry means to move rapidly with short quick steps.

Network as a noun means a group or system of interconnected people or things. The squirrels in this story have their own network, and when they use it to communicate, they are **networking** (verb).

Musical Terms:

Melody: Pitches that form the main part of a song.

Keys: In music, there are major (happy) and minor (sad) keys. Composers choose major/minor keys to help describe feelings and moods through music.

Camp Resound
Boomer's Tales: Book 3
A Preview

"Chloe," Nana Weathers said, "please put Boomer in his pet carrier and fasten the seat belt over it so he'll be safe. You and Shannon can sit in the back seat together. Boomer will be my co-pilot."

"Okay," Chloe said, "but you'll need to t-teach him how to read a map." They both laughed.

Before climbing into Nana's car, Shannon hugged her parents who had dropped her off. As her parents started their car and pulled out of our driveway, Shannon waved to them and shouted, "See you at the Finale Concert in a month."

We were off on an adventure together. The New Hope Elementary School festival had raised enough money to send two students to Camp Resound. Chloe and Shannon were the two students from New Hope who'd been chosen. I was coming along as a mascot. I'd become known as the "singing dog" ever since the school's talent show. Nana Weathers had been asked to accompany the camp's chorus. She'd also volunteered for kitchen duty. In her words, "You all know how much I love to cook!"

"I hope we'll be in the s-same cabin," Chloe said to her friend.

"Me too," Shannon said. "I'm so excited to take flute lessons and play in a chamber group."

"I'm excited about singing in the c-chorus."

"I hope we'll have hamburgers, hot dogs, barbecue, and fried chicken to eat," Shannon said.

"Ooh, and ch-chocolate ice cream with sprinkles on top—my favorite."

They laughed.

All this talk of food had made me start to drool. Nana Weathers said, "Boomer, I brought along some of those famous Pet Friend liver treats you like.

She didn't have to tell me, though. I'd already sniff, sniffed them in the food bag with my kibble.

Shannon said, "I brought my swimsuit so we can go in the lake."

"It's called Lake Promise," Nana Weathers said. "There are also hiking trails nearby. Although you are both going to have full schedules, there will be time for activities other than music. An excursion to a special place has been planned. For now, though, it's a secret."

"That s-sounds like fun!" Chloe said. "Hey, let's play a game, Shannon. You, Nana, and I can come up with a n-name for our car. Does that sound like fun?"

I yipped, "I like that game."

Nana Weathers said, "I'm driving and need to pay attention to the traffic. You and Shannon come up with some names."

"Since your car is blue, you could name it Blue Thunder," said Shannon. "My dad used to have a Thunderbird when he was younger. He showed me photos. It was red and silver and very shiny. He told me it could really go fast. Since your car can go fast too, I like that name."

"Me too," said Chloe. "I was thinking of the name B-bluebird. It's my favorite bird; I love to hear it s-sing and watch it fly."

"I like that name too," Shannon said.

"I've g-got an idea! Let's call the car Bluebird Thunder. That puts our car n-names together. Is that okay, Nana?"

"I give it a blue ribbon; it's a winner. Well, here we go! We're at the turn off for Camp Resound."

"I can't wait," I yipped.

About the Author

Christine Isley-Farmer's second book in her series, "Boomer's Tales," continues the adventures of a Cavalier King Charles Spaniel as the story's narrator. Christine loves this dog breed and has owned three Cavaliers. She encountered her first Cavalier, Fleur, while performing with the Harrisburg Opera. She was captivated by the big brown eyes and gentle, lively nature of the breed. Her present Cavalier, Dylan, likes to walk with her, chew on his favorite treat-stuffed Kong toy, and snuggle next to her in a recliner. Christine, a classically trained singer who has sung professionally in the United States and Europe, has also been a voice teacher. The stories in opera and song have fascinated and inspired her. The power of stories and music's healing qualities have woven their way through her life and have found voice in her writing.

CPSIA information can be obtained
at www.ICGtesting.com
Printed in the USA
LVHW051232021121
702213LV00002B/245